We might not see the wind, but we can feel it on our skin, and we can see the things that the wind blows around.

The wind blows falling leaves from the trees.

It makes swirling patterns in the crops.

The wind spreads the pollen that gives some of us hay fever.

pollen

It ruffles animals' fur.

**This dog is very windswept!**

Over time, a strong wind can even make trees permanently bent.

The wind can blow at different speeds. Wind speed and strength is shown in knots. Different wind speeds are given different names as well.

**Q** Look at the wind scale below. What is a wind with a speed of 70 (seventy) knots called?

| Wind speed | Name |
| --- | --- |
| 4 to 6 knots | light breeze |
| 7 to 21 knots | breeze |
| 22 to 27 knots | strong breeze |
| 28 to 40 knots | gale |
| 41 to 55 knots | strong gale |
| 56 to 63 knots | storm |
| 64 to 120 knots | hurricane |

**A** It is called a hurricane.

Satellites can show us what a hurricane looks like.

Hurricanes can uproot trees, smash windows, and strip roofs from houses. Very strong hurricanes can even lift cars and buildings off the ground!

a hurricane

In a hurricane, the winds twirl around and can cause a lot of harm.

Sometimes, a hurricane can make a whirlwind (or twister). A whirlwind is a narrow funnel of wind and cloud that is swirling very quickly. Like hurricanes, whirlwinds can do a lot of harm.

Whirlwinds can pick up dust and small objects, and blow them around.

Even a weak wind can shape things.

These rocks in South America have been shaped by the wind. It takes a very long time for this to happen. As the wind blows, it picks up small bits of sand and dust. The sand and dust then rub against the rocks to make these odd shapes.

wind-blown rock

The wind shapes and smooths the sand dunes in a desert as well.

Sometimes, a strong desert wind picks up a lot of sand and dust, and forms a sandstorm.

**dust clouds**

It is very unpleasant to be stuck in a sandstorm.

We can see which way the wind is blowing by looking at windsocks or weather vanes.

A windsock is a big fabric tube attached to a pole.

The wind blows in one end and out the other.

The arrow on a weather vane shows us which way the wind is blowing from by pointing to a letter. The letters stand for **N**orth, **S**outh, **E**ast and **W**est.

Knowing which way the wind is blowing is very important for sailors who use the wind to sail their boats.

**wind**

Sailors steer their boats by shifting their sails from side to side. They can even sail into the wind by tacking (zigzagging along). Tacking is a difficult skill to learn.

**tacking**

Many sports would not be possible without the wind. Windsurfing and kitesurfing are just two of them.

Windsurfers have a sail attached to a surfboard. The sail catches the wind and makes them speed across the waves.

kite

Kitesurfers use a kite and a surfboard. The wind in the kite drags the kitesurfer along.

Like kitesurfing, ballooning and kite-flying would be impossible without the wind.

Did you know that a balloon cannot be steered left or right? A balloonist can take off and land, but when the balloon is in the sky it goes wherever the wind blows it.

Children and adults have been flying kites for a very long time. Kites are even shown in cave paintings from thousands of years ago!

**a rainbow kite**

The wind helps trees and flowers to spread their seeds. The seeds of many trees and flowers are just the right shape to catch the wind.

These sycamore (/**sic**emor/) seeds are thin and flat at the ends. They look like helicopter blades when they spin around.

Ash tree seeds are thin and flat, too. Their lightness means that the wind can carry them a long way.

These dandelion (/**dan**delieen/) seeds have little bristles at the top. The bristles act like a sail or a kite to catch the wind.

Did you know that the wind can carry dandelion seeds up to 95 miles away from the flower? That is a long way for a little seed to travel!

Did you know that we can use the wind to power things?

The first windmills were invented more than a thousand years ago in what we now call Iran.

Windmills use the power of the wind to crush wheat into fine flour. The wind spins the sails, which turn the cogs, which turn the millstone that crushes the wheat into flour.

sails

cogs

millstone

The wind powers the many Dutch windmills (or wind pumps) that line the canals in the Netherlands. They were built in around 1740 (seventeen forty) to drain the land so that it could be used to grow crops.

Some of these windmills are still used to stop the canals overflowing onto the land.

We still use the wind to power things today.

This is a wind farm, with lots of wind turbines. Each turbine has three blades. As the wind blows, it spins the blades around and around. This makes electricity (/elec**tri**sɛtee/), which we can use to power anything electrical, such as laptops and tablets.

a blade

Wind power is very good for the planet. Other ways of making power, such as burning coal, pollute (harm) the planet, but wind power does not.